SA012059

821.008

PET

1 WEEK

Poems With
Attitude

Andrew Fusek Peters
and
Polly Peters

HODDER
Wayland

CONTENTS

SEXUALITY 59–71

BOOZE AND DRUGS 73–91

Dedications

To Isdall School, whose year 10 booking began this collection, and in loving memory of my brother Mark Edward Peters. A.F.P.

To John Masefield High School. P.P.

SNOGGING

snog v. & n. Brit. slang.

– v. intr. **(snogging, snogged).** engage in kissing and caressing.

– n. a spell of snogging. [20thc.: origin unkn.]

Where were the experts when it came to kissing?

Her boyfriend had broken his leg. Time to get rid of him.

She asked if *I would be the one for her*.

I lied about my age. She believed me.

I was over the moon. In fact, I was over the whole planetary solar system.

Now, I had to kiss her!

Real kissing. Not just that smack on the lips from gran stuff.

Some business to do with tongues. Oh, I knew that, tongues.

It's what we sniggered about at the bus stop. . .

Tongues touching! Revolting or what?

I couldn't remember if I'd cleaned my teeth. She was smiling,

Ready for a great big smackerooni!

I felt like James Bond with wet socks.

Can you do tongue warm ups? Lip practice?

No going back now. This was it.

I was the stone that fell off a cliff. And her lips?

Well, I know I'm being poetic really,

But they were soft like the sea and I went splash.

Wow! Mmmmm!

Now all this was wonderful, but her friends were sitting on the bed

Watching us like an experiment. Completely off-putting

There were several words I'd like to have said, but this is a polite poem
And anyway, they were her friends.

Back to the kissing.
Technically speaking, our mouths were swapping spit,
And our tongues rolled round like wrestlers.
I found it hard to breathe.
It was great.
Five minutes went by. Then another five. Then another.
You get the picture.
Limpets were wimps compared with us.
Half an hour now.
Her eyes were closed. She seemed to be enjoying it.
I began to panic. My tongue was drowning.
What if it died?
I mean, all this kissing wasn't too bad, but I was exhausted.
Two hours later (I promise this isn't a brag, well not totally)
We finally ripped our lips apart and said goodbye.
I wandered round the town
With my tongue lolling out like a dog.
This must be love!

Unfair Fiona

On holiday in Verona,
I fancied fair Fiona,
So gorgeous now I'm blown a-
Way by thoughts of you!

But she met a boy who'd shown her
His biceps tanned with toner,
Now he's frenching my Fiona,
I'm a loner with nothing to do!

Got home and tried to phone her,
No answer for she's goin'a-
Way with that hunky moaner
On a Vespa built for two.

Farewell my false Fiona,
My heart it needs a donor,
I feel like a jilted Jonah,
Wailing and oh-so blue!

Kiss in slow motion

GLOSS APPLIER

CHAT REPLIER

FLIRT CATCHER

WINK SNATCHER

LIP CRUNCHER

POUT SCRUNCHER

MOUTH MASHER

TEETH GNASHER

TONGUE HOPPER

SALIVA SWAPPER

MOMENT'S MAN

IN THE CAN

HER ADORER

TOUCH RESTORER

STROKE SURPRISE

WIDENED EYES

HAND SNAKER

RULE BREAKER

DOWN BELOW

NO GO!

Goldilocks & the Phwoar Boys

(after: We're Going On A Bear Hunt)

We're going on a boy hunt!

We're going to catch a good one.

We're not scared!

Uh Oh! Spots!

We can't go out with them. We can't get over them,

We'll have to just cover them!

DIBBY DABBY DIBBY DABBY DIBBY DABBY SPLAT!

We're going on a boy hunt!

We're going to catch a good one.

We're not scared!

Uh Oh! Hair!

Just can't cope with it! Can't get around it!

We'll have to comb through it!

FRIZZY TANGLE FRIZZY TANGLE FRIZZY TANGLE OW!

We're going on a boy hunt!

We're going to catch a good one.

We're not scared!

Uh Oh! Breath!

Can't get over him, Can't get off with him,

Got to mouthwash!

GARGLE GURGLE GARGLE GURGLE GARGLE GURGLE BELCH!

We're going on a boy hunt!

We're going to catch a good one.

We're not scared!

Uh oh! Clothes!

Gone over everything, Can't get into it!

Have to go through them all again!

ZIP SNAP ZIP SNAP ZIP SNAP RIP!

We're going on a boy hunt!

We're going to catch a good one.

If only we dared!

Uh Oh! Make-up.

Foundation under, blusher over it,

Looking gorgeous through and through!

BRUSH BLUSH BRUSH BLUSH BRUSH BLUSH CRUSH!

We're going on a boy hunt!

We're going to catch a GREAT one.

We'll be paired!

Uh oh! Mum!

No way over this, can't get round her,

She'll see through me.

FLOUNCE SLAM FLOUNCE SLAM FLOUNCE SLAM

DAMN!

Connected

I love my dialling darling
Where roads have come to meet,
And she has got me cornered,
In the phonebox down the street.

Although it's not too roomy,
I'd recommend the view,
This palace of naughty numbers,
But the one that counts is you.

I'm afraid it's damp and drafty,
But love's a breezy catch,
I dream of our hands cupping,
The centrally heated match.

I feel like a beeping fool,
Disconnected, dumb, deranged,
Fumbling my coin of words,
Hoping for a little change.

For she has come and changed me,
It took one simple look,
And I'm desperate to receiv'er,
Don't leave me off the hook.

My eyes are frosting up now,
My heart's a broken pane,
My home the lonesome phonebox,
Under the ringing rain.

Bus Stop Date

Night makes a fog of fagsmoke
And love stains nicotine,
Each kiss dragging on our lips,
My menthol, matchless queen!

Waiting Game

Outside the swimming pool at six.

Just enough light to check my reflection, breathless, pulse doing a four-minute mile. Lungs like bellows, fanning the fire that blooms on my face when I see my Mum's best friend. "Hiya Love. Waiting for a friend? Oooh, a lad is it? Nudge Nudge!" Thank God she's gone. Look at watch. Five minutes early. Damn. Not cool to be here first. Force hand with watch to swim in pocket, but it's like my wrist is pushing down a float. It just wants to pop up and keeping my arm down is like pushing down a drowning child: Unthinkable! Whip it out and check for signs of life. Shake. No, it hasn't stopped. But if my watch isn't dead, then Time must be. Quick! Call an ambulance! Time has had a heart attack. There isn't any time to lose!

Four minutes to go. Try not to look too eager. Lean against wall and rearrange legs with all my weight on one foot. Do I look casual enough or like a scrawny flamingo? Maybe pink wasn't the best choice. Should I go home and change? Then I'd be late. Though late is cool, and then he could stand and wrestle with *his* watch. But then he might think I wasn't coming and go home, and I'd never see him again and grow old and die alone in a bedsit in Bangor. No, best to stay.

Three minutes. I'll saunter over and read the notices. Oh God! Didn't realise I was staring at the poster for Aqua Ante-Natal classes. Did anyone see?

Two minutes. Get back to the safety of the wall. My friend, the wall. Me and Mr Wall, tall, dark, handsome and concrete. Hanging out with a gang of bricks. Hard as houses. Yeah. Got to have something to read. Wish I'd brought a magazine. Hurray! an out of date bus timetable in the oasis of my pocket.

One minute. Check reflection. Does my hair look OK? It wasn't frizzy this morning. Zap! Pow! Biff! FRIZZ! Why can't it be curly like Katrina's? If only I had a cleavage, I'd be a knock-out! Count of ten, nine eight. . . Clock tower chimes the hour. Where is he then? Don't want to be seen looking out for him. Pretend there's something really interesting in my bag. He's set me up, and all the others will be laughing at me in the morning, I know it. They'll call me Kate In Wait, Sad and Snogless! It's all a big joke to him. He hates me. He hates me. He hates me. "Oh! Hiya Matt!"

What my mother said

My mother always used to say,
When I sat sobbing at tea,
"Don't worry my girl, you're gorgeous!
And there's plenty more fish in the sea!"

"Now wave him goodbye, he's far too shallow,
Just trust, you'll have what you wish!"
"Well, thank you so much for your helpful advice,
But I couldn't get off with a fish!"

Holiday Romance

I was just twelve, and she, thirteen,
Our tongues went round like a washing machine.
Our smooching broke parental law,
A slurping kiss that left lips sore!
Romantic, adventurous holiday,
Snogging and sandcastles, if only she'd stay!
When I went home, I wrote her verse,
Her letter back was cold and terse;
Said I'd love her until the earth ends,
But she replied, "Let's just be friends!"
And oh my heart, how it still bleeds
For Sharon Smith who lived in Leeds.

FAMILY

family n., pl. **-lies.**

1. a set of parents and children, or of relations, living together or not. . .

. . . 5. a brotherhood of persons or nations united by political or religious features.

[ME f. L *familia* household f. *famulus* servant.]

Silence and Smiles I

I left some crumbs in the butter
A frown spread across his face.
It was teatime.
My stepdad fell utterly silent.
This was a personal insult.
The house died. No radio, no TV,
Just the song of his sighs, heaving like some ham actor.
My stomach churned.
It was almost funny.

On the fifth day,
He blessed me with his bank manager smile,
Gave me a greeting that was all sickly cream,
And I smiled back,
Desperate to please the man
Slowly curdling my mother's heart.

Smiles and Silence II

I was his little sugar and spice,
And had to call him Daddy.
He required a buttered up kiss at morning and night,
For a fifteen year old, it was creepy.

It was teatime.
I had brought home my boyfriend,
Had no desire to kiss a bogeyman.
My stepdad fell utterly silent.
This was a personal insult.
The house sighed. No radio, no TV,
Just his melodramatic breath, gasping in and out.

My boyfriend mumbled excuses and left,
Skimming off all the good feelings of the day,
Leaving me sour as old milk.

Smiles and Silence III

He had his little act off pat.
When guests turned up,
He was all voice, oily-smooth as margarine.
The door closed, he turned into a slab.
My mother moved into the spare room.

It was teatime.
The house was silent. No radio, no TV.
Every little bit of us was tidied away.
I came in, looked around,
Saw a pair of black tights sprawled across the bed
And knew, just knew he had finally strangled her.
Until I heard her car outside.

That night,
I climbed the hill above town,
A fog melting the pale yellow light,
And looked down
On the tidy houses filled with suffocating families,
And wondered if they too were practising
Smiles and silence.

The Customer

"Mind your own business!" said the wild-eyed man,
Breathing into my flabbergasted face.
"It's the holidays!" joked the wife, "a bit of fun!
You know what kids are like, all over the place!"
She cried, carried on serving me,
Tried to hide her bruises with make up and made up lies,
As if I had not seen what I had seen:
A boy in a necklock with fear in his eyes.

I spoke up, perhaps a foolish bravery,
Me, the stupid, do-gooding customer
Then left, leaving a madman even more angry.
Later, behind blind doors, drink would father
Another punch, one son grow to know and run
Father's business, hitting his wife, beating his son.

Too Late

"Now don't come back beyond midnight."
My only reply is to swear.
How dare she tell me what to do!
The fact is she really does care.

"And leave me the telephone number."
I wish she'd get off my case,
But mum is concerned for her son,
Who just wants to get off his face.

When I stagger back beyond midnight,
She cries "Can't you see that I worry?"
I try not to giggle, get out of her sight,
In the morning, perhaps I'll say sorry.

Look at my power! I've made her cry!
Now I'm a man in the making!
"I love you," she said, but I laugh instead,
So why does my heart feel like breaking?

In the end I try to make up,
Invent some fairly white lies,
One day, I'll tell her everything,
"If only we'd talk," she sighs.

Oh Dadless me and Sadness Mum,
Somehow we just rub along.
"We'll make the best of the worst," she smiles
And home is where I belong.

There is no magic in him

There is no magic in him,
Only the magisterial father,
Falling like crumbled brick
To his unmuscled eyes.

There is no magic in him,
Nothing he can do right
Except to be shovelled,
Mixed up and finally tough.

At school, he stirs,
And fills the hours with "No!"
If the system is his father,
Let it try and beat him,
Let it!

But there is no magic in the bricked up boy,
Turning away all lesson and proverb.
The Song of Solomon is sour in him,
Betrayed by fists,
He would pass on that betrayal
Before the clock struck break.

Be a fisherman,
Catch him with words, for a while.
Cast on the waters with a sweetness,
And he squirms from that uncarping touch,
Slips free the magic in him.

And the smile is a first edition,
Lips cut open in grace,
And all that is hate
Now crumbling.

But home is a phone,
Reminding him to stay in touch
With what he knows,
Where distance is a closed shop,
And the hammering of static
Beats all magic from him.

Terse Rima

(In Memory Of Frederick Maxwell Peters)

I am the thief who has taken a life!
Sang the man as he bowed most graciously,
And fell to earth, widowing his wife.

It was a case of perfect electricity,
The spark that stole you sudden as a blade,
Cutting the ties of fear and family.

My mother found you in a forest glade,
Your arms flung up as if in prayer,
Free from pain at last. But the price you paid

Was us, stolen away from cuddle and care
Sentenced to years of solitary grief,
For a husband and father no longer there.

Drink was an accomplice, the friendly thief
Who snatched my hoarded pain away.
When recovered, it was beyond belief,

A priceless hurt that came to stay.
This precious love I lack is large as life,
And every waking day is Father's day.

The Trigger (after: Blake's *The Tyger*)

STATISTIC: Ten young people of school age in the UK commit suicide each year due to being bullied

What the trigger? What the cause?
Was it words with sharpened claws?
And did the tiger smile to see
The lamb now running fearfully?

What the thought that prowled inside
The dream of doubt that never cried?
What the hammer? What the chain?
Beating out the forge of pain?

When the sick and startled stone
Made to snap the gentle bone,
What the moment? When the time,
Broke the breathing of your rhyme?

And who to shoulder your dead heart,
When you have played the final part,
Leaving those with torn out sight,
Grieving in the grove of night.

Facts and Fiction

I was told to jump by a hidden voice
Which whispered that I had no choice
To follow the footsteps of drop Dead-Dad,
Had all the requirements, stoned and sad.
I might as well give it a try,
Flap my arms, like Icarus, fly.
Dear reader, it's obvious I wasn't jolly,
But completely off my trolley.
All those years of trying to hide
Swagbags of feeling stuffed inside.
The bullies, trained in taking the peace,
Were the secret emotion police;
Arrested anyone for showing tears,
Sentenced the sensitive to years of fears.
Those voices now, I realised,
Were just the bullies, internalised.
I wrote a note that said *toodle-oo*
And shuffled up a step or two.

The fire escape led into night,

And I looked down with sudden insight.

Though my life was utterly shitty,

The mess below would not look pretty.

If this is what you contemplate,

Then take it from me, it's better to wait.

And though each day seems a pain in the arse,

Remember my friend, This Too Shall Pass.

Horse of Night

Horse of my blackest addiction,

I have felt your blood

race

the quarter mile between

my head and my heart,

and I have cheered you on,

and died at the starting gate,

and run with you,

with my heart in my mouth,

my whole body

miles down the road,

and I have collapsed,

spent

at the broken gate

you crossed

to gain your freedom,

and you dragged me on,

on a race no one could win,

racing for racing's sake,

racing until your hard, proud,

black veins pumped dry,

and the sun

and moon

bowed to your hard body,

and today is tomorrow

and I am racing still.

By Mark Peters (1961–1993)

For Mark

For when my brother dies,
I shall cry tears of stone,
Never will I have felt so alone
And my heart will try to be hard.

For when my brother dies,
No more late-night Monopoly and after
Bacon and eggs with a cup of laughter,
The yolk of dawn just breaking.

For when my brother dies,
I shall cry a city of tears
Then put on a smile, hide all my fears,
If only I could, if only.

For when my brother dies,
No more hate and family spite,
Now I'm fine, everything's all right
But I will miss the making up.

For when my brother dies,
I shall cry blades of grass,
People will be polite, dare not ask
Why my garden overgrows.

For when my brother dies,
I shall have no brother,
No other to hug and to hold
And I the younger
am the one who will grow old.

High up in the Hills

High up in the hills
The wind is blowing my brother away.
He is going away now
As if he was just popping out to the shops
As if he just put the phone down
As if he went for a walk and just carried on.

I remember the tale of the Alcoholic who told his wife
He was just slipping out for a packet of cigarettes
And wasn't seen for five years.

My brother is not migrating like a bird
Nor is he folding over the world like the moon,
To grow thin, disappear and come back new again.
He is no fairy tale
For in the story, they live happily ever after.

He doesn't have a writer's block.
There is nothing more to write
And all there is between us are the memories we made.
So shall the days go.

He is dying of Aids.
But who is there to aid him in this death?
A midwife for life...
Who shall bring him out? Who shall give death to him?
Ease him in his labours, his dying pains?

Who shall husband him, mother to him, hold him?
And shall he cry out like a newborn babe?
Cry out against the shortness of his years,
The tight span he squeezed to the last breath
That ended by squeezing him?

No answers,
For answers only come at the end.
And no one is going the whole way with him.
It is his death. He must own it.
He must die it.

And if there is light,
Why is it so full of darkness?
And if there is faith,
Why can I only question?
And if there is peace,
Give him some,
That he may sleep.

FRIENDS

friend n. **1.** a person known well to another and regarded with liking, affection, and loyalty; an intimate. **2.** an acquaintance or associate. **3.** an ally in a fight or cause; supporter. **4.** a fellow member of a party, society, etc. **5.** a patron or supporter: a friend of the opera **6. be friends (with).** to be friendly (with). **7. make friends (with).** to become friendly (with). ~vb. **8.** (tr.) an archaic word for **befriend.**

[Old English *freond;* related to Old Saxon *friund,* Old Norse *frandi,* Gothic *frijonds,* Old High German *friunt*]

Sometimes it's all so amazing

Sometimes, it's all so amazing,
I could fall at the feet of every singing pigeon.
Shopkeepers' conversations seem positively Shakespearean
And the sweet wrappers that flower down the street
Are perfectly arranged.

Sometimes, it's all so amazing,
I could watch a tree like a TV,
Every leaf an amazing documentary,
Each shadow riveting as a World Cup final.

Sometimes, it's all so amazing,
I'd say kind things to people I can't even stand,
Look for the good in their face, heart and hand,
And find it.

Sometimes, it's all so amazing,
Every day becomes a holy day,
I could even pray to bacon and eggs!
And a cup of tea is a spiritual experience.

Sometimes, it's all so amazing,
I could say hello to a complete stranger,
Let go my forever fear of danger,
And just for a second he would become my deepest friend.

The Horror, the Horror!

Out to my mate's for a night in, that's terminally groovy,
Got loads of crisps and coke in for the x-cert horror movie.
Give us a gory giggle (Yeah!), and snorts of sudden surprise,
For the close up, slowed down scene, where they gouge out
each of his eyes!
We never turn away (No Way!), nor hold our popcorn breath,
As we love spurting blood (Hooray!) and dollops of dastardly death!
Cycling home at the end's alright, except for the dark bike shed,
Where a psycho waits just out of sight, to slowly remove my head!

He and she

We were best friends, a fit like kettle to cup,
And the boiling need to brag and boast was poured away.
We talked as fast as a racing horse, every word a winner.
I dug into my pocketed fears,
A kid showing his precious marbles,
But the only thing she laughed at was my doubt.
She praised my sky-scraping dreams,
High rise hopes in a young head.

One night, we wandered backstreets,
Infatuated with neon, addicted to architecture.
Tipsy with talking, we swayed through busy avenues,
'Til we came to a churchyard crushed in a corner.
All was sweet and silent,
Save for the murmur of a million shifting feet.
An old street lamp splashed yellow into shadow.
A fat oak tree squatted like a leafy Buddha,

And gravestones kept themselves to themselves,
Their stone epitaphs seeping into green.
We sat on the wall, between present and past,
Best friends for now and for now and forever now,
Where the cobbles were pearls beneath our feet.

Perfect Blend

She's a:
Sadness safe-cracker,
A down-in-the-dumps hijacker.
A deepest secret keeper,
A talk-for-hours non-sleeper.
An automatic advice dispenser,
A future candidate for Mensa.
An Olympic-qualifying talker,
A hold-head-high-whatever walker.
A listener to all my woes,
A fear-of-God to all my foes.

A promise fulfiller, gossip killer,
Dance-all-nighter, tiredness fighter,
Solid shoulder for things I've told her.

She's my:
Round the bend, got to spend
Quick to lend, own trend
Perfect blend
Best friend!
(what would I do without her?)

1 Slugs & Snails & Puppy Dogs' Tails

Lads like football, lads like cars,

Lads like hanging round in bars.

Lads fart to start up conversations

And hang in gangs at railway stations.

Lads show off by acting tough,

And don't know when they've drunk enough.

Lads love lager with designer labels,

But end up legless under tables.

Lads like playing contact sport,

And wear the socks their mothers bought.

Lads play rugby, lads play pool,

But often don't do well at school.

Lads wear T-shirts when it's chilly

With no idea that they look silly.

Lads can't cook and Lads can't sew,

They'd rather sit and watch grass grow.

Lads, you know, are king-sized rats

However I can tell you that's

A load of crap from where I'm sitting,

'Cos I'm a lad who's into knitting!

2 Sugar & Spice & all things nice

Girls are sugary, girls are spicy,

Girls like trainers that are pricy.

Girls like pink and fluffy stuff,

Girls are sweet and don't act tough.

Girls wear high-rise, platform heels,

Girls theorise on how love feels.

Girls like boys, and girls like dates,

Girls like shopping with their mates.

Girls keep secrets from their mums,

And like to eye up cute boys' bums.

Girls like talk that lays souls bare,

Girls like to style each other's hair.

Girls are friends 'til death do part,

But steal their bloke and you're a tart!

Girls like gossip, girls like bitching,

Snipping friendship's careful stitching.

Girls compare who they have kissed,

Girls can wound without their fist.

Girls read books about romance,

And step round handbags when they dance.

But this girl thinks this list is barmy,

'Cos she's just off to join the army!

Bullying

bully ~n., pl. **-lies. 1.** a person who hurts, persecutes, or intimidates weaker people.

2. *Archaic.* a hired ruffian. **3.** *Obsolete.* a procurer; pimp. **4.** *Obsolete.*a fine fellow or friend.

5. *Obsolete.* a sweetheart; darling.

~vb. **-lies, -lying,-lied. 6.** (when tr., often foll. by *into*) to hurt, intimidate, or persecute

(a weaker or smaller person), esp. to make him do something.

~adj. **7.** dashing; jolly: *my bully boy.* **8.** *Informal.* very good; fine. ~interj. **9.** Also: **bully for you, him,** etc.

Informal. well done! bravo!

[C16 (in the sense: sweetheart, hence fine fellow, hence swaggering coward): probably from Middle

Dutch *boele* lover, from Middle High German *buole,* perhaps childish variant of *bruoder* BROTHER)

Remembrance Day

When we have left our school in peace,
Does bullying's shellshock ever cease?
Here's a rollcall, the sensitive few,
Names called out in the blameless crew:
Mandy the fat one, without any hope,
At last succeeded with a length of rope;
Yaseen, shamed for her boot-black skin,
A gallon of bleach did her in;
James, too posh for the common attack,
Went over the top with a hit of smack;
Martin Martini, skinny git,
Gave up eating for the hell of it.
Thanks to the bullies, bayonet in hand,
Leaving us in No-Man's Land,
Privates fighting private thought,
Trying to ignore what we've been taught.
And me? Retreated in the warmth of dope,
Got too blown away to cope,
Wondering what the hell it's for,
Limping, survived the mindless war.

Now, I am a veteran, visiting schools,
Who doesn't take kindly to thuggish fools.
They think it's a gas, don't see that their fun
Is the equivalent of a loaded gun.
I'm so sick of sickos taking the piss,
Deserting their conscience in cowardice,
Leaving the lost ones with lonely fears,
Trudging the trenches of tear-sodden years.

Ray

Summer thinks he's a lad,
Though it's all a flowery farce
In fact when he drinks, he's a total rain
And the sun shines out of his grass.

Unevensong (sung by the stupid)

To the tune of: What shall we do with the drunken sailor?

What shall we do with Duncan Taylor?
What shall we do with Duncan Taylor?
What shall we do with Duncan Taylor
Early in the morning?

Hoo-ray and up he rises!
Life is full of cruel surprises!
And we're several sizes
Bigger than him this morning!

Lock him up in the classroom cupboard!
Lock him up in the classroom cupboard!
Lock him up in the classroom cupboard!
To serve him as a warning!

What shall we do with Duncan Taylor
Now he's become a stinking wailer?
This is the life of a teenage jailer,
Early in the morning!

Laugh at him when he starts to weep,
Got what he asked for, little creep,
Can't say that I'll lose any sleep,
When I rise in the morning!

What shall we do now he's sunken paler,
Call him a sissy girly failure,
Works too hard, it's time to nail 'her',
Serves him right for fawning!

Laugh until our guts are aching,
Stupid prat what a racket he's making,
By God it's fun to be taking
The rise in the early morning!

Hoo-ray and up he rises
Life is full of cruel surprises
And we're several sizes
Bigger than him this morning.

Bruises Heal

Names, cold shoulders,
Silence in the canteen;
Her words are scalpels,
Cutting self esteem.

"Stuck up little cow!
Thinks she's really it!"
Laughter slices, she prescribes
A sharp, unfunny wit.

Ridiculed for standing out,
My marks are much too high
And so she drip-feeds saline hate,
Injecting with a lie.

She's bright, she'll find
The weakest spot to pierce and prod and poke.
She uses stealth, and poisoned words
And wears them like a cloak.

It seems I am her favourite game
And I'm the one who loses,
If she'd done this with her fists,
At least there would be bruises.

Camp Concentration

At school, if your hair was too long,
Or if you weren't particularly strong,
If you were sensitive to names,
Or quiet, or not into games,
They called you *bent*, *poof*, *queer*
And gave you the gift of a life of fear.
Once their limited vocabulary was spent,
Not fitting in, you were branded different.
These childish rules equally applied
If you were fat, or thin, or easily cried,
Or white, black, brown, not part of the race.
Losers, wore glasses on their face.

The Nazis came from that same school,
For them it was a gas to apply the rule,
Narrow-minded, upright, straight,
Twilight thugs, handing out hate.
My mum, when twelve, in Prague one night,
Had the SS search her room by torchlight,
Boots so high they reached above the bed,
"Looking for resisters," they said,
As they took her school friend far away,
On a camping trip that none would choose.
I have friends who are gay,
My mum had friends who were Jews.

"Waiter there's a thug in my salad!"

I'm an apple,
Used to hang round with a bunch of grapes.
The Hard Bunch, but they all ended up as winos.
Now I'm in the apple gang.
Wanna be in my gang?

For a start, we don't like oranges.
Any orange that gets in our way,
We squash! You should see them run!

Lemons? Yellow through and through,
Not as tough as me or you.

Lychees? Oh please!
They're a funny colour, and they're foreign.
Go back to Lychee Land.

Bananas? You must be bananas!
Fruit cakes all of them! Bender Boys.
Don't wanna get mixed up with that bunch.

Pineapple? What can you say?
I mean, zits or what!?
You could almost peel her skin.

She needs help badly!
Onion? What are you doing here?
Don't you know you don't belong?
Send for the doctors!
He's a total vegetable case!

Who does that leave?
Melony Melonbrain,
She's a pain, she's too fat,
Too soppy, too sweet
And she's soft in the head.
I think you're better off dead, my dear.

Pears? My older brother's a pear!
So pears are alright! Alright?
In fact, he's so hard,
He'd have YOU for breakfast any day!

'Cos I'm a happy apple with all my apple friends.
If you wanna belong,
Don't be a lemon, or a stupid melon!
Just put on an apple skin and sing my apple song!
Apple! Apple! Apple! Oi! Oi! Oi!
Apple! Oi! Apple! Oi!
Apple! Apple! Apple!
Oi! Oi! Oi!

Building Blocks

I have been built out of bullies,
With insults they moulded me.
For a while I walled up my fears,
And hid myself in poetry.

The house of books where I wandered,
In rooms of brain-bright thought,
Sheltered me brick by tender brick,
And the hateful words they taught

I caught and made my own
confident concrete tower,
To look down on the bullies,
For the pen is a mighty power.

They laughed at the sensitive boy,
And his guttering, spluttering tears,
But bottled up bullies get old and cold,
As they blunder the lonely years.

Oh bully boys that built me,
Don't you know that girls find appealing
Not louts who love to get plastered,
But boys filled up with feeling?

Yes, I was the prat that was good for a laugh,
The skinny old git, the swot.
Now I'm living my life with a beautiful wife,
Free from the bully dry rot.

So thank you, bullies that built me,
With all your crumbling hate,
Out of this mess, came a success,
And a man who has mastered his fate.

Sexuality

SEXUAL adj. 1. of or relating to sex, or to the sexes
or the relations between them.
2. *Bot.* (of classification) based on the distinction of sexes
in plants.
3. *Biol.* having a sex.
sexuality n. **sexually** adv.
[LL *sexualis* (as sex)]

Girl Talk

Now most people think that a poem might deal
With the shimmering swaying of trees,
So a subject you may not expect in a verse
Is sexually transmitted disease.

Discomfort! Shock horror! You can't discuss that!
We want love poems, something romantic!
But horror and shock are inadequate words
If it's you who are suddenly frantic.

Diseases with names I can't even spell
Are more common than most people know,
And a sudden encounter, an intimate match,
Is all that they need to grow.

In the heat of the moment, when starting to feel
Swayed by his shimmering eyes,
Remember that trees are never immune
From being cut down to size.

Remember the brother who couldn't be bothered
With barriers or thoughts of protection.
He just wanted some fun at the party, and thus
Gave that virus a welcome reception.

A dearly loved son, a brother, a boyfriend,
A lad who adored pretty maids.
"Cut down in his prime," wept his friends, when they heard
Of the loss in his fight against Aids.

Now trees have hundreds and thousands of seeds
And a mission to multiply,
"But I'm not a tree! It won't happen to me!"
Is the stupidest kind of lie.

So if it's your choice and you've made up your mind,
Don't leave this decision to luck,
If he won't use a condom, ignore all his charms and
Forget it, he ain't worth a. . .

Diagrammatic

My mum gets dead embarrassed
By my questions, which have her floored.
She told me that a diaphragm was:
"What the teacher draws on the board!"

I shouldn't have asked my dad,
With his terrible sense of timing,
But at dinner he tried to explain
That tampons were "essential for climbing."

I asked my mum about the pill,
And was it dangerous to take?
She shook her head, then smiled and said:
"It's great for a bad headache!"

Oh meet my ignorant family,
Repressive, evasive and quiet,
For this girl, it's about bloody time
To start an Awareness Riot!

Nothing to prove

It was a case of tender lust, when talk turned to touch,
Her detecting fingers gently fussed,
Forgave my frantic fumbling clutch
In case of tender lust.

My mum was out, her bed became a must,
Our sighs were sirens, nothing was too much,
Until the springs surrendered,
The bed was bust!

Her words dissolved my impotent fears. Such
Love now sentenced me to trust,
Jailing doubt as out of touch
To close the case of tender lust.

PS: My mum is still annoyed about the bed!!!

Gas Mark 16

I'm really tired of being told about sex
By ancient, mouldy, pain in the necks.
If it's so bad, how come I find,
That certain thoughts keep crossing my mind?
And adults do it, but never say,
Else how did I get here anyway, eh?
But boys are bad, with their wicked wiles,
Their lying hands and deceiving smiles.
I won't be served with this stereotype,
Send it away with its overdone hype!
For love is a recipe, followed with care,
Seasoned with feeling and flamed until rare,
And whether they're fast-food fish and chips,
Or a slow-cooked tender steak, relationships
Don't have to be a drunken alley slam,
Or a five-minute fumbling Wham Bam.
And don't worry, we're not all dumb,
I've taken advice as a rule of thumb,
Protection's a starter that saddles this horse,
Before we ride out to the main course.
Then there's time to enjoy and explore –
The secret of the adults' swinging door
That they want to keep slammed shut.

But I am not some adolescent smut-
Obsessed lad (though, maybe that's a lie!),
Corrupting girls with a wink and a sigh,
Nor am I some deadly depraved beast,
But merely a beginner at life's fruitful feast
So come on, give us a break, don't quibble,
Just because I crave a natural nibble!

What goes on in boys' heads

Oh Tanya, my darling tomato-haired totty
I tried to Ketchup, but you gave me the slip.
In my dreams you are saucy and ripe for some hotty,
But then you turned round and gave me the pip.

Pressure

Have you? Haven't you?

Do you? Don't you?

Will you? Won't you?

Who is going to?

Peer Pressure, Peer Pressure

It could be fags, it could be fashion,

Could be drugs, it could be passion.

Peer Pressure, Peer Pressure

Love it, loathe it, like it, hate it,

No escape, must just await it.

Peer Pressure, Peer Pressure

Boys, they have to brag they've scored,

Build the lie 'til mates applaud.

Fears Pressing, Fears pressing

Girls get stuck in two way traps

In murky mazes without maps.

Jeers Press Her, Jeers Press Her

If she does, she's called a slag,

And rumours build with tongues that wag.

Peer Precipice, Peer Precipice

But if she doesn't, which is worse?

"Tight Bitch!" is the poisoned curse.

Sheer Pressure, Sheer Pressure

But, we're given brains to reason things,
Don't have to wait for what fate brings.
Clearly Precious, Clearly Precious
We have a mind, we have a choice,
We have an individual voice,
No need to put your life on loan,
It's no one's choice except your own.
Peer Pressure, Peer Pressure
Peer Pressure EXPLODES!

Mind Pollution

Though the hairstyle resembled an oil spill,
His chatup, well slick was the word.
But his bragging was crude as he went for the kill
And fouled this particular bird.

If only he'd talk to her once in a while,
Instead of just dropping his anchor,
A lumbering vessel without any style,
Now he's known as an absolute tanker.

Statistic: "70% of young women regret their first sexual experience"

It was way back in the sixties:
A right was battled and won,
By women who fought for freedom of choice
Beyond that of mother or nun.

Now we're forty years further,
But more trapped than ever, it seems
For belief in choice has broken
Like the mirror of childhood dreams.

For the right to say "Yes" got hijacked,
Somewhere along the way,
To become just a foregone conclusion
No discussion, no choices, no say.

And it's "Loaded minx, She's desperate for sex!
Read all about it inside!"
And, "Be one of us!" the insidious chant,
"Don't end up on the opposite side."

Perhaps it's time for a different cause,
A fight for the right to say "No."
And to be well informed, learn more about choice,
And to know that it's fine to go slow.

It's active choice that should be the crusade,
Responsible, reasoned and yours,
Not passive, or pressured, assumed or presumed,
For you hold the key to those doors.

Information is power, it means you can choose
The right person, right time and right place.
Then there are no regrets for you've opted to take
The slow journey, and not the fast race.

Easy

He swaggers downstairs and stops
To see who might be looking, hesitates
And joins a group who loll against the wall;
Drags attention from a fag burn in the carpet
By dramatic adjusting of his shirt,
Then squats. "Got a fag?" he asks,
Grinning deliberately, willing them
One of them, to ask: "Where is she then?"
Only a slight exhalation indicates relief at being asked.
Slowly, he draws a breath,
Like the drumroll preceding the high wire act
And rolls his eyes.
"Upstairs y'know. Sortin' herself out."
And he smiles a lazy smile
And hooks his thumbs in belt loops,
Stage whispers, "First time y'know: hers, not mine of course."
And his audience lean back appreciatively.
"Where's that fag then? Gotta light?" Deep drag now.
"Well, yeah, bit of a slag, but a goer. Oh yeah! A real goer."
They are reeled in, staring and envious.
"Did you really?"
"Oh yeah, too right!". . .

While upstairs,
Mascara tears
Rain black
Into the basin.

Booze & Drugs

booze *n. & v. colloq.*

– *n.* **1.** alcoholic drink. **2.** the drinking of this (on the booze).

– *v. intr.* drink alcoholic liquor, esp. excessively or habitually.

[earlier *bouse, bowse*, f. MDu. *busen* drink to excess]

drug – *n.* **1.** any synthetic or natural chemical substance used in the treatment, prevention, or diagnosis of disease. Related adj.: **pharmaceutical.**

2. a chemical substance, esp. a narcotic, taken for the pleasant effects it produces.

[C14: from Old French *drogue*, probably of Germanic origin]

The Pearls of Primrose Hill

That night, her son got drunk,
Stole a bike and wove his way
In giggling stitches through the fraying streets.
The leather-black air was sharp,
And his breath, a swaying incense
As he prayed to the god of speed.

He hit the hill at sixty,
And took to the trees in a slalom,
Wild boy-rider, tilting at windmills,
Mistook a bin for his enemy and charged.
Took flight,
True as the compass needle,
Dead-head butted the unforgiving litter.
His front teeth burst like buttons,
Limp as cloth, he fell to the ground.
Thank god for Anaesthetic Alcohol,
His mouth a rose now blooming with blood,
The ragdoll son crawled home.

His mother was waiting, waiting

Waiting all the long and solemn night.

When she saw him,

It punctured her pincushion heart.

She sped him in a hurry to the hospital,

Where experts informed her that teeth could be saved.

At the comedown of dawn,

The sudden grey woman

Crawled through dogshit grass,

Carrying such unbelievable grief

As she searched the hill for needles in the haystack,

The precious pearls of her son's smashed teeth.

On Hampstead Heath

The moon is round as our wide eyes.
We lounge in the living room of grass,
With friends as soft, breathing pillows,
And flickering lights of the city below
The image we are glued to.
Fresh picked mushrooms mash in our mouths,
Mixing with jokes and salty whispers.
Joints passed like salt and pepper,
Condiments for conversation.
We breathe in honeysuckle, roses, stocks;
Hold the high until our lungs almost burst with the
Scent of summer.

Night grows deep as thought,
We are dozy starlings, anxious for the nest.
We slip into the tarmac river with our skateboards,
Swoop and slalom down hills with a hiss,
Past dumb cars, shut-eyed windows and
Lamps drowsily nodding their heads.
We lean into corners and turn, the wheeling flock
Moving like mercury
As we tumble into the valleys
Of fumbling locks and stumbling stairs
And the easy contentment of sleep.

War Story

Couldn't find a vein, what the heck,

Stuck the needle in my neck.

Felt the beaming sun fantastic,

Heart slowed down, eyes elastic.

Hours of nodding, gouging out,

One of the gang raised up a shout:

"Oh dear, O'Malley's OD'd!" she said.

He wasn't just pale, but rather dead.

"What shall we do with him now?" she cried.

With totally smacked out brains we tried

To think of a plan that was truly cunning,

Though all we felt like doing was running.

We said a little junkie prayer,

Then rolled him up in a rug threadbare.

The house was a wreck, the builders' chute

Provided an excellent exit route.

I'm afraid that while we giggled away,

O'Malley slipped down like a fast bob-sleigh,

And landed, crashed out in a council skip.

It was that kind of relationship.

I'm ashamed to admit that we found it a scream,

And O'Malley? Gone like a darkening dream.

Black

It was night. We were stoned with lagered-up skinheads
On the roof of the shell of a squat
In the warm summer city.
Our laughter rippled,
Though the friends-of-a-friend thugs in boots and braces
Seemed too quiet.
The youngest started it, demanding our dope.
Not more than thirteen,
Face smooth as a chilling cherub
He swung his pendulum fist.
My brother's white shirt turned red,
A magic trick gone wrong,
His head dealt blow after blow from the pack.
I curled into the corner, a fragile new moon,
And the pounding made me see stars;
Their grunts and our groans, sounded almost pornographic,
But my only desire was to fly.
Adrenaline grew me wings,
I soared from the screaming roof.
Neighbours stayed quiet behind a flock of locks –
As I landed, ran through the light-shy lanes
Desperate for mum.

For years after,
I escaped into Kung-Fu movies,
Imagined I'd been training since I was six,
Relished encounters where gangs were wiped out
With a flick of a finger
And an enigmatic smile on my boyish face.

Fag Off

When at school,
Fags were cool.
Not so young,
Removed right lung.
Hacking got to me,
Tracheotomy.
Ignore that boffin!
Carry on coffin'.
Finally led
To a boxed in bed,
Nobody's fool,
I'm now *dead* cool.

The Night Kitchen

The Mohican has lost his America.
His hair cuts the air like a scythe.
Tonight is his night.
He stoops in the subway and finds ten pounds,
Hey! Food and fags and glue,
To stick together what has fallen apart inside.

He squats in Islington,
Burning furniture for fuel,
Squeezes his glue into a plastic bag,
Then like the horse this Indian never rides,
He puts his face to the trough
And snorts the heady fumes.
His mane quivers, eyes roll,
Radios blare in Pentecostal tongue
And the fire is in his head.

Mohican canters into the streets,
Searches out oases dead by day
And breathes in the midnight hour.
Offices have closed their mouths,
Are dumb to the shifters and shufflers,

And Mohican, eyes spinning like plates,

Juggles legs and arms in the effort to remain upright.

Night is swift as lark,

And sharp shop windows filled with women bring no comfort.

There is nothing to be had,

But the comedown of the moon,

Sagging like an old breast,

And the mole stars fading in the twilight.

Cleaners come in trucks, on foot

To fill the silent city with broom and bustle.

Curtains itch. Alarms declare bad jokes.

And the coffee shops reveal a drinking hole.

Mohican slows his trot to a walk and seats himself in the saddle

of caffeine.

The rising of the sugar salmon

He slips out,

Lost in the singing crowd,

Moving against that rush hour ride,

Searching for the source in what dark spring.

Pub-erty

It wasn't all fights and vomit and death.
To be tall was a blessing. Take a deep breath,
Walk up to the bar, and ask for a drink,
Landlord sees boy with bottle, doesn't blink,
But pulls the pint, and I set up, set sail
Fifteen, skinny as a yard of ale.
Sudden found friends, and spilling ease,
I was part of the gang on the high seas
Of lager, laughter, perched on my girl's knee,
In the harbour, safe from her storming family.
The evil that got her dad was not *this* drink
That he hid in bottles under the sink.
This couldn't be the stuff we swore we would not touch,
But glue that bound us, careless crutch
Of liquid warmth on winter nights,
Gambling the fruits and flashing lights,
Far, far away from drowning school,
As we dived on cue into games of pool.

When the bell rang, like froth we poured
Into the streets, suddenly cold and bored,
Tipsy weavers, threading the gloom,
Headed with take-outs for somebody's room,
And dancing, kissing, gulping down fun,
The black and tan night only just begun.

Bored

When I was a teenage thug,
Before I discovered the arts,
We'd hang around the bikesheds,
Smoke fags, and light our farts.

Blow-Back

Grass, Blow, Dope and Spliff,
Red Leb and oily Black,
These are the words that turn you on,
To a night out on the crack.

Bong, chillum, paraphernalia,
Pipes and skins galore,
Laugh, giggle, got the munchies,
Rolling round the floor.

Boy with hash has instant mates,
Whose smiles are filled with lies,
Shallow hero of the night,
With double-glazing eyes.

Strangers, nonsense, garbled words,
Head bent over the loo,
Rush slowed down to a sickly trickle,
Spaced out, splash and spew.

Got so high, went into orbit,
Planets of pills to pep me,
Hot sweats, visions, paranoia,
Police are out to get me.

All this fun for the price of a toke,
That made me a real hard lad,
But in the end I lost the joke
And went completely mad.

Oh people who take drugs are cool,
In school, they've got street cred,
But personally, there's more to life,
Than ending up dull or dead.

Icarus Sickarus

I was nervous,
They suggested a drink
Gave in, said yes, didn't think.

I felt less shy,
They said you could try
One puff of this, and boy you'll fly!

I was gliding,
Didn't take heed,
When they said Sniff this! you'll be up to speed.

I took off
Towards the sun,
Burn this! they hissed, It's a ball of fun!

I took it,
Until I could take no more,
Suddenly began to soar,

The sky was melting
I jumbled my words,
That fell like tumbling come-down birds.

I crashed,

And suddenly woke to find,

I had mashed the wings of my mind.

Sniffing for glues

Give a squeeze

Liquid frees

In the bag

Make me gag

Such perfume

Head goes ZOOM

Sticky nose

Vision grows

Sky rise hum

Down I come

Thirteen floors

Thunder roars

End of story

Rather gory

Mad for it

I could not get used to the habit,
My mind worn away with using,
Lost in the waves and foaming mad,
Too far from Normality Shore,
Stuck in Sargassos of saddening weed,
As the tide shut me off like a door.

I was too shy to walk through the door,
As a youth, had developed a nervous habit,
Until I was offered a toke of weed,
Could not be seen to be refusing,
One puff, and Wow, I felt so sure,
Confidence soared, I talked like mad.

Bullies are puffed up and mad
On fear, So I hid as a kid behind the door,
Hoping for a teacher to reassure
Me. They didn't. I was left to inhabit
A school where hate was a musing
Scythe to cut this pathetic weed.

So I became best mates with weed,
It grew in me and I grew madder,

Blossomed into dark abusing.
The Lord of Hash was the one to adore,
I prayed at the shrine in my punk-rocker habit,
Visioning monk of the cocksure.

On one last trip I left that shore,
So stoned, I lost control, weed
Myself, shat the floor, was led to the habit
Of hospitals, and wards of the wingless mad,
Lived in fear of the locking door
Could only mutter, "It's so confusing,"

Over and over, all thoughts fusing
Into a lump of black. I tried to shore
Up my sanity, but the greedy Jackdaw
Had stolen sense to feather his widow-weed
Nest. Me the March hare, dancing mad,
Broken down, shuffling out of habit.

This was the joy of using weed,
A boy marooned on the maddening shore,
At last his habit of dope unhinged him,
slamming shut the hopeful door.

Is there life after drugs?

Without the drugs I felt naked and raw,
Unsure of winning this personal war.
I wouldn't go back, but couldn't see,
That getting clean was victory.
I remember once, stoned on a train,
Overheard this couple, with half a brain,
Talking about how drugs were boring,
As they stared into each other's adoring
Eyes. It made me want to puke, and how
I laughed at those poor saddos. Now
I fit this anorak myself,
Have left the pills on memory's shelf.
The first time I made love, in fear
And lack of faith, I tanked myself on beer
And rolled a spliff with shaking fingers.
This is the image that lingers;
No girl had seen me naked before,
Would she laugh at what she saw?
Thank God that fear was left unfounded,
Only my out-of-it brain was confounded.
Life today without the boozy bandage
Is much more fun. Perhaps it's age,
But somehow pissed-up Friday nights,

The blur of clubs and lure of neon lights,
The chat ups, the endless mindless mumbling,
The stagger, the sway, the feel up fumbling
Is over, done. When I was barking, out of my tree
Friends and future were a fantasy.
Easier to fly on feather white coke,
And laugh at life's great big bloody joke.
So off my head, I nearly lost the thread.
Friends of mine succeeded, wound up dead
Cool? No, truly cool is taking a toke of life, a puff
Of late night love is more than enough.
Sometimes I laugh so much, I'm totally gone,
And strangers ask what is he on?
Nothing mate. The world is my upper,
I'll do without that liquid supper.
Jacked up with hope for the days ahead
I chase the dragon of my dreams, instead.

Index of first lines

It wasn't all fights and vomit and death. 82

Lads like football, lads like cars, 44

"Mind your own business!" said the wild-eyed man, 23

My mother always used to say, 16

My mum gets dead embarrassed 62

Names, cold shoulders, 52

Night makes a fog of fagsmoke 13

"Now don't come back beyond midnight." 24

Now most people think that a poem might deal 60

Oh Tanya, my darling tomato-haired totty 65

On holiday in Verona 8

Out to my mate's for a night in, that's terminally groovy, 41

Outside the swimming pool at six. 14

She's a: 43

Sometimes, it's all so amazing, 40

Summer thinks he's a lad, 49

That night, her son got drunk, 74

The Mohican has lost his America. 80

The moon is round as our wide eyes. 76

There is no magic in him, 26

Though the hairstyle resembled an oil spill, 67

We were best friends, a fit like kettle to cup, 42

We're going on a boy hunt! 10

What shall we do with Duncan Taylor? 50

What the trigger? What the cause? 29

When at school, 79

When I was a teenage thug, 83

When we have left our school in peace 48,

Without the drugs I felt naked and raw, 90

About the authors:

Andrew Fusek Peters is an author, editor and broadcaster. His poems have been regularly heard on Radio 4 and he was a presenter/writer for the BBC1 children's poetry series 'Wham! Bam! Strawberry Jam'. He has edited four Hodder-Wayland anthologies including a collection of shape poems called *The Upside Down Frown*. His books have gathered excellent reviews: "A hugely enjoyable, original collection," said the T.E.S. of *Sheep Don't Go To School*; the *Guardian* named one of Andrew's books of stories for young children their Children's Book Of The Week.

Andrew's last major collection *May The Angels Be With Us* was written with his brother, who later died of AIDS. It was widely praised: "A powerful collection" (T.E.S.); "unique" (Brian Patten); "Very moving poems" (Kaleidoscope).

Apart from writing, Andrew is constantly touring schools and literary festivals, running workshops and giving performances. He was recently on a North Sea gas platform as poet-in-residence for the Poetry Society.

Polly Peters is a former English and Drama teacher. She
was previously Head of Drama at a sixth form college and
currently works as a youth/community theatre leader, director
and playwright. Her last collection of plays, *Czech Tales*, has
recently been published, and she has collaborated with
Andrew on *The House That Learned To Swim*. Andrew and
Polly live in a converted chapel in Shropshire with their
daughter.

First published in 2000 by Hodder Wayland,
an imprint of Hodder Children's Books

© Andrew Fusek Peters and Polly Peters 2000

Prepared for Hodder Wayland by Mason Editorial Services
54 Exeter St, Brighton BN1 5PH

All rights reserved
Printed in Hong Kong.

British Library Cataloguing in Publication Data
is available for this title.
ISBN 07502 22847 4

Hodder Children's Books, a division of Hodder Headline Ltd
338 Euston Road, London NW1 3BH

MORE POETRY FROM HODDER WAYLAND

The Poetry Collection:
Themed collections by Brian Moses & A.F. Peters, illustrated by Kelly Waldek. 27 x 22 cm, full-colour, 32 pages: £9.99 hardback and £4.99 paperback.

Poems About Animals   *Poems About Space*
Poems About Festivals   *Poems About School*
Poems About Food
Poems About Seasons

Poems About Me/Poems About You and Me:
Poetry about what it means to be a member of society. 27 x 22 xm, full-colour, 32 pp: £9.50 hbk & £4.99 pbk.

ALSO AVAILABLE AS BIG BOOKS:
44 x 36 cm, £13.99

The Worst Class In School, Brian Moses (ed.) 1999.
Also:
The Upside Down Frown, A.F. Peters (ed.) 1999.
I Wish I Could Dine With A Porcupine, Brian Moses, 2000.
The Boneyard Rap And Other Poems, Wes Magee, 2000.

Poems About:
Themed collections of poems for young children. 27 x 22 cm full-colour, £4.99 paperback only.

Poems About Families
Poems About Feelings
Poems About Journeys
Poems About Weather